Play the Game

Baseball
& Softball

Play the Game

Baseball & Softball

Paul Gregory

WARD LOCK

Half-title page: *The excellent technique of pitcher Kevin Brown of the Florida Marlings makes it difficult for many batters to score*

Title page: *Gotcha! A baseman successfully tags and puts out a runner before he reaches his next base*

Above: *Batter Jose Canseco in full flow during a match at the Oakland Coliseum in California*

Contents

Introduction

Baseball and in its variants have become the ball game played by mixed groups the world over as an easily-staged, enjoyable and competitive social activity.

In the face of strong competition from other sports, baseball has retained its popularity and continued to justify prime-time television slots across North America, where it is at its strongest. The professional game still draws big crowds to stadia throughout the United States and Canada almost every night of the week. The atmosphere of a live game attracts the supporters despite national TV coverage and the diverse sporting menu offered by the small screen. Star players are heroes, the leagues competitive, newcomers are microscopically studied and veterans of the game revered and adored by the numerous fans.

At college and university level the game is professionally organized and enthusiastically sponsored with the media eager to chart the progress of young players through this 'feeder' system. Earlier still, in the parks and yards, most American youngsters – and others around the world – take up a bat and ball at a very early age and start out in a sport which many stay with for life.

Baseball is now a world game. It is played in more than 100 countries on five continents across the globe. The International Baseball Association (IBA) governs the sport internationally, running the world championships every four years. Baseball has also been a full Olympic sport since 1992. Cuba won Olympic Gold in the 1992 and 1996 games; however the IBA has now allowed professionals into competitions, so watch for the United States and Japan in future.

Like soccer, baseball and softball benefit from the minimal cost required to create a game. A basic baseball field can be marked out on almost any surface and spare area of ground; with bat, ball and players you are up and running. Once you have thrown your first pitch, struck your first run or taken a high catch, you will want to play again, and again.

The *Play the Game* series offers a basic introduction to a sport and explains its origins and history, its equipment, terminology and rules, before offering the fundamental tuition required to acquire a rudimentary skill. Master the essential techniques and your talent for the games of baseball and softball will increase. Whether it is sufficient for you to play your modest part in a social team, or plan to advance to a higher level, your first step in these wonderful sports will be more certain, more confident once you have used *Play the Game: Baseball* as your guide.

Enjoy the game!

History & development of baseball

Just who is responsible for the birth of baseball? The English claim that it derived from the very English games of cricket and, more likely, rounders.

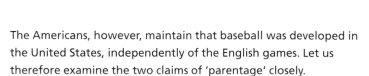

The Americans, however, maintain that baseball was developed in the United States, independently of the English games. Let us therefore examine the two claims of 'parentage' closely.

The earliest known reference to rounders was in 1744 when J. Newbery's *A Little Pretty Pocket Book*, published in London, contained a woodcut of the game and was captioned with a verse entitled 'Base-ball'. This book was definitely published at least twice in the United States before the end of the eighteenth century.

A description of the rules of rounders was included in *The Boy's Own Book* in 1829 and many features of the game were common with those of baseball. The distance between bases in rounders are somewhat shorter than in baseball but the shape of the playing area is similar, with the bowler (pitcher in baseball) taking up a similar position. So far, then, everything points to baseball stemming from rounders.

That is the English claim to being the founders of baseball. Now for the American case.

Oliver Wendell Holmes is believed to have played baseball at Harvard University in 1829 after reading a copy of *The Boy's Own Book*. He is said to have modified the playing area into a diamond shape.

But there is another claimant: a West Point cadet called Abner Doubleday, who asserted that he had laid out the first diamond-shaped pitch at Cooperstown, New York in 1839. He maintained that he invented the game spontaneously, and without any knowledge of rounders. But that was ten years after the rules of rounders appeared in *The Boy's Own Book*, so can his claim be taken seriously?

It is known that 'base ball' was played in both England and America in the early eighteenth century, but we have already established that 'base-ball' was the forerunner of rounders. The question that needs to be answered is: was 'base-ball' also the forerunner of baseball?

Needless to say, England and America each continued to maintain that they had invented the game, and a special commission was set up in the United States in 1905 to try and establish when and where baseball was really born. They found in Doubleday's favour and declared that baseball was born at Cooperstown, New York in 1839.

The first basic rules of the modern-day game were drawn up by a surveyor, Alexander Joy Cartwright junior, on 23 September 1845. Not only did he draw up the game's first twenty rules that day, but he also founded the Knickerbocker Base Ball Club of New York, the sport's first organized team … it was a busy day for Cartwright!

Prior to Cartwright's rules the most popular version of baseball was the Massachusetts game, in which a player was out if hit by a thrown ball! Cartwright abolished this rule and introduced the tag rule instead. But his most important innovation was the introduction of the three strike rule.

The first match under Cartwright's rules was played at the Elysian Fields, Hoboken, New Jersey on 19 June 1846, and the Knickerbockers were humiliated by twenty-three runs to one by the newly formed New York Base Ball Club.

Other clubs sprang up in no time, particularly in the northeast, and on 10 March 1858 twenty-five clubs formed the first baseball league, when the National Association of Amateur Base Ball Players was established. It was not long before the game became commercialized, and on 20 July 1858 some 1500 spectators paid 50c to watch Brooklyn play the New York All Stars at Long Island's Fashion race course, in the first game to command a paying attendance.

Professionalism followed and in 1869 the first wholly professional team, the Cincinatti Red Stockings, was formed, with players averaging $890 in the first season … the rewards for top players were high even in those days. The man put in charge of assembling the Red Stockings was an Englishman, Harry Wright. Born in Sheffield, he emigrated to the United States as a youngster and later joined the Knickerbockers before taking over as player-manager of the Red Stockings. He is regarded as the father of professional baseball.

With the development of professional teams it followed that a professional league would be born, and on 17 March 1871 the National Association of Professional Base-Ball Players was formed as a result of a meeting on Broadway, New York. The Philadelphia Athletics were the first champions but the Boston Red Stockings won the next four championships, before the league folded amidst scandals of match-fixing, heavy gambling and drunkenness among the players. Baseball was at rock bottom, but Chicago businessman William Hulbert was determined to resurrect it and restore it to its former glory.

Hulbert formed the National League of Professional Base Ball Clubs in 1876. That same National League still thrives today despite the challenges of other Leagues over the years. One of Hulbert's first regulations restricted the franchising of teams only to towns or cities with populations of at least 75,000. The new league also prevented players from moving from one club to another during the season.

A rival American Association was set up in 1882 and in 1890 a third league threatened to disrupt baseball when the National Brotherhood of Professional Players formed a league.

With three leagues in existence baseball was in a financial mess. Trade wars existed between the teams and the leagues, but after only one season the National League absorbed the Professional Players League. Barely a year later the American Association folded, and peace reigned for a decade – until the turn of the twentieth century.

Another trade war and internal struggles within the National League in 1903 led to their recognizing another new league, the American League, which had been set up in 1901 by Bryon 'Ben' Johnson. The two leagues fought each other for two years but in 1903 settled their differences and signed an agreement to control Organized Baseball. Those two leagues still exist today in the United States.

A third league, the Federal League, was formed in 1914, but the big two leagues fought it and it survived only two years.

Baseball developed rapidly as a spectator sport in the 1920s, and the old wooden stadiums were pulled down to make way for new larger concrete ones. Fans poured in by the thousand to see such great names as Walter Johnson, Ty Cobb, Lou Gehrig and, the greatest of them all, Babe Ruth. In 1987, more than fifty years after he retired, Ruth topped a poll of 10,000 readers of *USA Today* as the greatest sports star of all time. Furthermore, in that same poll, 58 per cent of readers said Babe Ruth's bat was the one piece of sporting equipment they would most like to own.

The biggest event in the US sporting calendar is the World Series, held in October. It is a best-of-seven matches meeting between the winners of the National League and American League. After a regular season consisting of 162 matches, the top teams in each League do battle in a knockout competition to see which should represent the League in the World Series.

First held in 1903, and won by the Boston Red Sox, the World Series has been dominated by the New York Yankees, who have won the title a record twenty-two times, thirteen more than the next best team, the St Louis Cardinals. Men like Joe di Maggio, Mickey Mantle and 'Yogi' Berra were the backbone of the great Yankees teams in the 1950s.

Professional baseball in the United States has had its ups and downs over the years, particularly as a result of political in-fighting, but it reached its lowest point in 1919 when a scandal broke over the 'fixing' of the World Series. The Chicago White Sox lost the series to the Cincinatti Reds, and eight members of the White Sox were found guilty of receiving bribes in what became known as the 'Black Sox Scandal'.

The man called in to help re-establish the credibility of baseball was Kenesaw Mountain Landis, a former Federal Judge, who was appointed the sole commissioner of Organized Baseball in the United States. One of his first tasks was to ban the eight White Sox players for life, even though a Chicago grand jury had failed to convict them in a farcical trial in which statements went missing and key witnesses fled the country! Landis remained commissioner up to the time of his death in 1944, and during his twenty-five years in office credibility returned to baseball.

By now you will probably have formed the opinion that baseball is entirely American. True, it is the national sport of the United States, and the professional game may have its roots there, but a very strong professional league exists in Japan, and many former US players are enjoying a second career in the Orient.

Japan is also a stronghold of the amateur game, and the Japanese beat the United States in the baseball final when the sport was introduced as a demonstration sport at the 1984 Los Angeles Olympics. World amateur championships have been held since 1938, and have generally been dominated by Cuba. Australia, West Germany, Italy and Holland are also strongholds of the amateur game, and it is growing in popularity as a spectator and participant sport in Great Britain.

Many people believe the game is new to England, but this is far from the truth. The first game of baseball in England took place in 1874 and was between two visiting American professional teams from Boston and Philadelphia. The British Baseball Federation was founded in 1890, and many soccer grounds staged baseball matches. Several clubs had their own baseball teams, including Derby County, Aston Villa and Orient. When Derby County Football Club moved from their original ground to the Baseball Ground, baseball was still played there and they carried on playing baseball and won the Championship in 1895.

During World War I, matches between American servicemen attracted a lot of attention. In 1924, at Stamford Bridge, Chelsea hosted a game between the Giants and the White Sox, which was attended by King George V.

Baseball in Britain enjoyed tremendous popularity just before

World War II when more than 700 teams played in various leagues and large crowds would attend the big matches. After the war, however, only pockets of the country maintained the sport, thanks to keen local enthusiasts; chief among these have been Merseyside, Humberside, Nottingham and London.

The success of baseball in the United States lies in its structure. The 'farm' system was introduced in the 1930s, whereby promising young players are assigned to minor league clubs owned by, or having a close relationship with, the major league teams. Budding young Babe Ruths, however, start in the Little League (Pony League, Babe Ruth League, etc.) and carry on playing right through high school and college. In the UK the British Baseball Federation in conjunction with Major League Baseball International operates a schools programme, Pitch Hit & Run. This programme is available to schools throughout the UK. The British Baseball Federation also runs leagues for senior and youth players.

Like soccer and cricket, baseball is an easy game to play in the local park. You need only a bat and ball and a bit of improvisation. Kids all over the United States start wielding a baseball bat as soon as they can walk. They all hope to emulate their own hero one day and become a star in their own right. Some make it. Some pass their dreams on to their children …

Overleaf: *Joey Cora of the Seattle Mariners practises swinging his bat near the on deck circle before batting against the Baltimore Orioles at Camden Yards*

Equipment & terminology

Baseball is a team game played by nine men per side. Play takes place on a field consisting of an outfield and infield. Within the infield is a 'diamond', and at each corner there is a base.

As baseball is a bat and ball game, the two principal pieces of equipment are, of course, the bat and the ball. However, because the ball travels at great speeds, protective clothing is required by certain players and officials, and all players wear gloves to help them to catch the ball.

Let us examine everything in detail.

The field (of play)
The baseball field is the equivalent of a quarter segment of a circle. An arc joins the two straight lines of the segment. The inner part is the infield and the remainder is the outfield.

The infield constitutes a 90ft (27.43m)-square diamond. The outfield is formed by extending two sides of the square. The lines

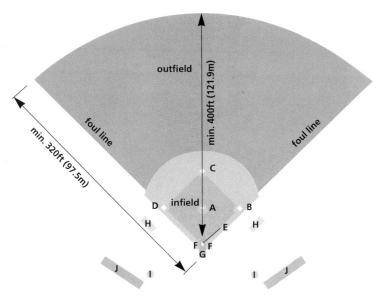

A: pitcher's mound
B: 1st base
C: 2nd base
D: 3rd base
E: home plate
F: batter's boxes
G: catcher's box
H: base coach's boxes
I: on deck circles
J: benches (or dugouts)

that extend from the square to the perimeter of the outfield are known as foul lines and should extend a minimum of 320ft (97.5m). The infield and outfield areas, including boundary lines, are known as fair territory. The area outside of the foul line is known as foul territory.

The pitcher has his own area of play within the infield, known as the pitcher's mound. At the top of his mound there is a plate, also known as the pitcher's rubber. Made of hard white rubber, it measures 24in (60.96cm) by 6in (15.24cm) and is set in the ground. The pitcher's plate is 10in (25.4cm) above the level of the home plate and the mound on top of which the plate stands is a circle with a 9ft (2.74m) radius. The distance from the front of the pitcher's plate to the back of the home plate is 60ft 6in (18.44m).

Home plate is the point which all runners attempt to reach after completing a circuit of all bases, in order to score a run. Home plate is situated adjacent to the batter's boxes and in front of the catcher's box. It is a five-sided piece of hard white rubber set into the ground. It is 17in (43.18cm) wide, and it measures 17in (43.18cm) from the front edge to the apex of the triangle formed by the intersection of the foul lines.

Players run from home plate in an anti-clockwise direction around the diamond, but must make contact with a base situated at

THE INFIELD

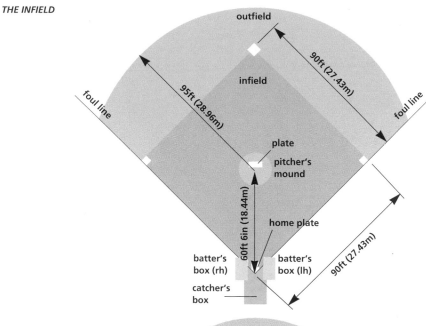

outfield

90ft (27.43m)

infield

95ft (28.96m)

foul line

foul line

plate

pitcher's mound

60ft 6in (18.44m)

home plate

90ft (27.43m)

batter's box (rh)

batter's box (lh)

catcher's box

THE PITCHER'S MOUND

Right: *'Bird's-eye view' – the shaded area represents the flat part of the mound*

Below right: *Front view of the pitcher's mound*

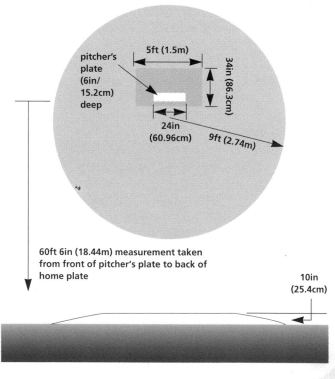

pitcher's plate (6in/ 15.2cm) deep

5ft (1.5m)

34in (86.3cm)

24in (60.96cm)

9ft (2.74m)

60ft 6in (18.44m) measurement taken from front of pitcher's plate to back of home plate

10in (25.4cm)

each corner. Each of the three bases consists of a canvas bag secured to the ground, 15in (38.1cm) square and 3–5in (7.62–12.70cm) thick, and filled with a soft material.

Coaching is allowed during play and coach's boxes are

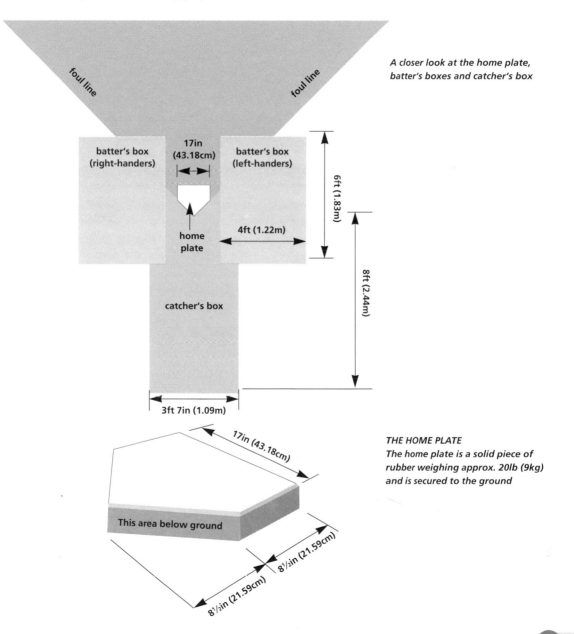

A closer look at the home plate, batter's boxes and catcher's box

foul line

foul line

batter's box (right-handers)

17in (43.18cm)

batter's box (left-handers)

6ft (1.83m)

home plate

4ft (1.22m)

8ft (2.44m)

catcher's box

3ft 7in (1.09m)

17in (43.18cm)

This area below ground

8½in (21.59cm)

8½in (21.59cm)

THE HOME PLATE
The home plate is a solid piece of rubber weighing approx. 20lb (9kg) and is secured to the ground

THE POSITION OF THE BASES
We have seen where home plate is in
relation to the diamond; the other
three bases are positioned as shown
here

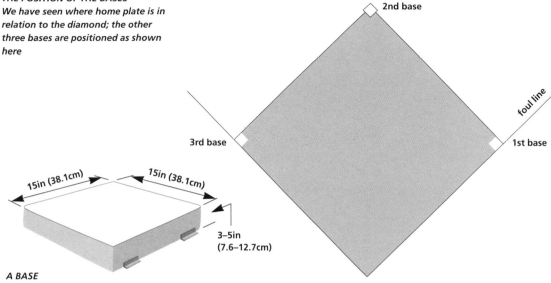

2nd base

foul line

3rd base

1st base

15in (38.1cm)

15in (38.1cm)

3–5in
(7.6–12.7cm)

A BASE
Each base is 15in (39.1cm) square,
made of canvas and filled with a soft
material. The bases are secured to the
playing area

ON DECK CIRCLES
Two circular areas, known as 'on deck
circles', are provided. The next man to
bat takes up position in the circle
before receiving his first ball. Each
team has its own on deck circle

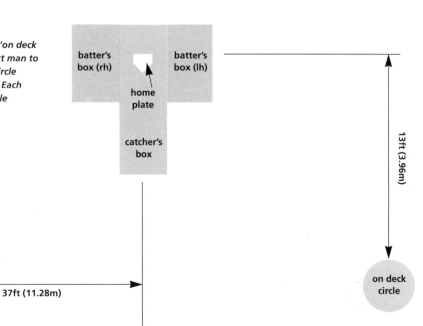

batter's
box (rh)

batter's
box (lh)

home
plate

catcher's
box

13ft (3.96m)

on deck
circle

37ft (11.28m)

on deck
circle

5ft (1.52m)

provided for the batting team's coaches and are situated by first and third base. Circles are also provided for the next batter in; these are called on deck circles and are situated to the right and left of the batter's box, and slightly behind it. Batters are advised only to swing their bat in the on deck circle or the batter's box. Swinging it at any other time could possibly cause an accident.

That is the playing area, now for the rest of the equipment.

The ball

The ball is round with a circumference of 9–9¼in (22.8–23.4cm) and should weigh 5–5¼oz (141.7–148.8g). It is made of yarn wound around a small core of cork, rubber or similar material, and covered in white horse- or cowhide. Deliberately damaging the ball (known as 'scuffing') is prohibited and offenders are severely punished, often with suspension.

THE BALL
The baseball resembles a tennis ball, as it has the same patterning, but is slightly larger and much heavier

The bat

The bat is best described as a smooth rounded stick, tapering from the thick part (the hitting area) to the narrow part (the handle).

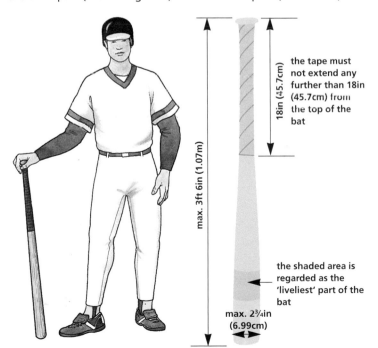

THE BAT
Left: *A regulation baseball bat*

Far left: *To put the size of the baseball bat in perspective, this is what it would look like alongside a 6ft (1.83m) tall player*

the tape must not extend any further than 18in (45.7cm) from the top of the bat

18in (45.7cm)

max. 3ft 6in (1.07m)

the shaded area is regarded as the 'liveliest' part of the bat

max. 2¾in (6.99cm)

The diameter at its thickest part should be no more than 2¾in (6.9cm) and the maximum length is 3ft 6in (1.07m). Bats are made of wood (ash) or stressed aluminium, although the latter is not allowed in Major League baseball. However, the aluminium bats are popular at amateur level, because they last longer than wooden ones.

The loading of bats by drilling them and filling them with cork to give them extra bounce is strictly prohibited. Sadly this practice has been carried out within the professional game in recent years and offenders have been punished severely.

The handle of the bat may be covered or treated with any material or substance to aid the grip, but most players prefer to wear a glove, similar to a golf glove, instead. If you put a grip on the bat, however, it must extend only 18in (45.7cm) from the top of the bat. The weight of bat is a personal choice but most are manufactured to around 28–32oz (800–900g). The liveliest part of the bat is about 6in (15cm) from the end.

Clothing

All players in a team should wear the same clothing and should each have numbers on their shirts.

Gloves

All fielders, including the pitcher, can wear a glove to assist with their catching. Gloves are made of leather and are well-padded but at the same time lightweight. They have a webbed pocket in which

GLOVES

Right: *This is a typical infielder's glove. The pitcher wears a similar glove, except that the webbing between the thumb and the forefinger is greater, to enable him to hide the ball from the batter*

Far right: *This is the first baseman's glove. In comparison to the infielder's glove it is more like a mitt*

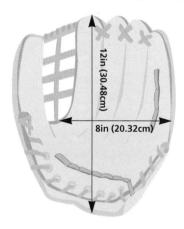

12in (30.48cm)

8in (20.32cm)

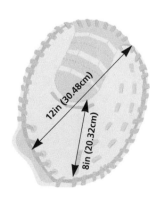

12in (30.48cm)

8in (20.32cm)

The catcher's mitt is held out with the palm of the hand facing the batter. This way the glove may be turned over quickly and the ball retrieved by the throwing hand

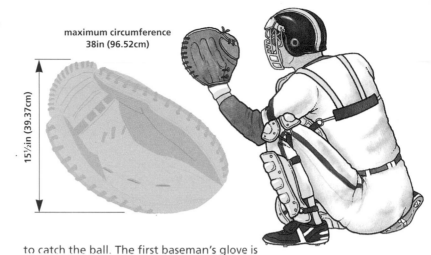

maximum circumference
38in (96.52cm)

15½in (39.37cm)

Protective clothing

to catch the ball. The first baseman's glove is often bigger than the other fielders' (except the catcher) and is more like a mitt than a glove. Other players wear gloves with the fingers laced together and with a webbed pocket between the thumb and first finger to aid the catching of the ball. The pitcher's glove is similar and may have extra webbing in order to hide the ball from the batter so he cannot see what kind of delivery the pitcher is going to make.

The catcher's glove is considerably bigger than other fielders' gloves. It can be up to 38in (96.5cm) in circumference and a maximum 15½in (39.37cm) from top to bottom. The catcher, because he stands in a dangerous position directly behind the batter, and faces balls coming at him at around 90mph (145km/h), needs not only a bigger glove but also extra protective clothing. Believe me, it's not funny being hit by a baseball travelling at full tilt!

Protective equipment

At one time the catcher used to stand a long way behind the batter because he had little protection. Now, with sophisticated lightweight equipment, he can stand immediately behind the batter and thus get involved in the action earlier. He wears protective headgear which incorporates a face mask, a throat protector, a chestplate and leg and ankle protectors. The home plate umpire, who stands immediately behind the catcher, also wears protective headgear and a chestplate.

BASEBALL CAPS
Right: *The conventional peaked baseball cap*
Far right: *A moulded plastic helmet with one ear protector*

Caps and helmets

The wearing of caps is synonymous with baseball. Batters wear moulded protective helmets while the fielders wear traditional canvas hats. The wearing of protective helmets by batters is now compulsory and the laws state that each must be fitted with at least one protective ear flap. Base runners must wear helmets to give them protection from a thrown ball.

SHOES
Below: *As you can see, the baseball shoe looks very much like a soccer boot*

Shoes

Shoes are lightweight and similar to soccer boots. Instead of studs they have either nylon, rubber or blunt metal cleats for use on grass surfaces. On artificial surfaces, however, shoes with moulded rubber-studded soles are worn. Spiked shoes, like golf or running shoes, are not permitted. Because they can be dangerous, shoe cleats are often not permitted in games involving younger players.

TERMINOLOGY

There are many terms in baseball, some are obvious, others less so. It is worth spending a little time learning them all.

Aboard A runner on a base is said to be aboard.

Assist A fielder who throws the ball to another fielder for a put out is said to have made an assist.

At bat A batter is at bat from the moment he takes up position in the batter's box until he is either out or leaves the box. A team is at bat if they have a batter in the batter's box.

Above: *The sole of the shoe, clearly showing that in this respect it differs very much from a soccer boot!*

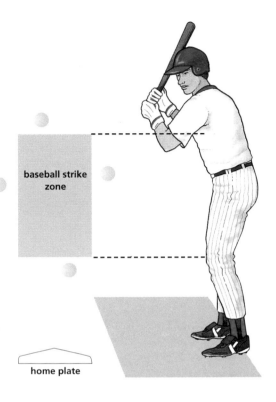

A BALL
All four pitches would in this instance be 'balls' because they are outside the strike zone

baseball strike zone

home plate

Balk An illegal act by the pitcher is a balk, and it entitles all runners on base to advance one base.

Ball A 'ball' is a pitch that does not enter the strike zone and is not struck at by the batter.

Base There is a base at each corner of the diamond. They are numbered in order: first, second, third and home plate. To score a run a runner has to complete a circuit of all bases in the correct order.

Base coach There are two base coaches in a team. One is positioned near to first base and the other near to third base. Their job is to give instructions to the runners. They operate from the base coach's boxes, as shown on page 17.

Baseman A fielder who guards one of the bases.

Base on balls If a batter receives four pitches outside the strike zone he is entitled to occupy first base. This is called base on balls, or a walk.

Batter's box The area of the field where the batter must stand during his time at bat is the clearly defined area known as the batter's box.

Battery The term used to describe the combination of pitcher and catcher, an important partnership!

Batting average A player's batting average is his number of hits divided by the number of times he bats. If a player receives a base on balls, is struck by a pitch or 'sacrifices' himself to advance a runner, then an 'at-bat' is not counted. It is calculated to three decimal places.

Bench The area of the park reserved for members of a team while waiting to join the game. Often called the dugout.

Bottom of the … 6th, 7th, etc. The second half of an innings.

Breaking ball A ball that changes direction while in flight.

Bullpen That part of the arena set aside for relief pitchers to practise in.

Bunt A bunt is a ball not swung at fully by the batter but tapped gently into the infield.

Catch A fielder makes a catch if he fairly and firmly secures the ball hit in the air in his hand or glove. A batter is out if a catch is made.

Catcher The catcher is the fielder who positions himself immediately behind the batter. He is the one who is heavily protected with chest, face and leg protectors.

Catcher's box The catcher must stand within the confines of the clearly-defined catcher's box until the pitcher releases the ball.

Change up One of the many throws in the pitcher's repertoire is the change up. He throws a slow ball but with the same action as if he were throwing a fast ball, thus deceiving the batter.

Count The number of balls received from a pitcher is called the count. The batter is allowed four balls or three strikes. The count is always made with balls first and strikes second.

Curveball A pitch that turns in to the home plate from the left as a batter in the right-hand batter's box looks at it (vice-versa for left-handed pitchers). A curveball also dips towards the home plate. (See pitching technique on page 56.)

Designated hitter In some competitions, designated hitters are allowed in place of a pitcher, who does not bat. His place in the batting order is taken by a recognized batter, who does not field.

Double When the batter reaches second base as a result of his hit he is said to have hit a double.

Double header Two regularly scheduled matches played in immediate succession are called a double header. Double headers occur often in major league baseball.

Double play When the defensive team put out two players as a result of one action they are said to have completed a double play. Obviously a desirable outcome!

Earned run average A pitcher's earned run average is the average number of runs scored off his pitching (discounting errors made by fielders) in comparison to the number of innings he has pitched in.

Error An error is committed when a fielder makes a mistake which would normally have put a runner out.

Fair ball A ball that is played into fair territory is a fair ball. A ball that is hit inside the confines of the playing area on the ground, but goes into foul territory after passing a base, is also a fair ball.

FAIR TERRITORY

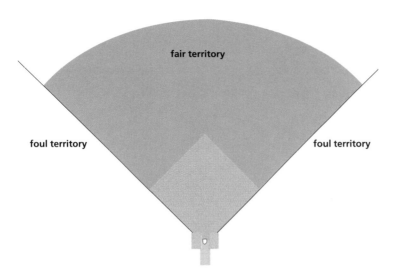

Fair territory The area of the field between the extended lines from the home plate through the first base and the home plate through the third base is fair territory.

Fastball One of the four basic pitches. The fastball is thrown as fast as the pitcher can deliver it. It travels in a straight line, but downwards towards the home plate. (See pitching technique on page 55.)

Fielder A fielder is a defensive player.

Fielder's choice When a fielder picks up a ball from fair territory and, instead of throwing it to first base in an attempt to put out the batter-runner, he throws to another base in an effort to put out a runner in front of him.

Fly ball A hit ball that goes high into the air is a fly ball.

Force play A force play is when a batter becomes a runner and the runner on first base has to give up his occupation of the base. If a player was also on second base in such a case, play would force him to move as well. No two players are allowed on one base at the same time.

Foul ball A ball that does not go into fair territory or one that goes into foul territory before passing a base is a foul ball.

Foul lines The foul lines extend from the home plate through first base to the perimeter of the playing area to form the right foul line, and from home plate through third base to the perimeter of the field to form the left foul line.

Foul territory Foul territory is that part of the field outside the foul lines, which extend to the first and third bases.

Foul tip A foul tip is a ball that touches the bat and goes into the catcher's hands and is caught legally. A batter is not out on a foul tip but a strike is called instead, unless of course it is the third strike against him, then he is out.

Full count When a batter has received three balls and two strikes.

Grand slam One of baseball's great sights is the grand slam, when a batter hits a home run with three players on the bases. He scores four runs for his team.

Ground ball A ground ball is a batted ball that travels along the ground.

Hack A wild swing by the batter that misses the ball.

Hit When a batter reaches any base after making a successful hit.

Home run A home run is scored when a batter completes the circuit of all four bases without stopping, as a result of one hit; also known as a homer. It is the equivalent of the 'six' in cricket, and it generally produces the same ecstatic response from the crowd.

Hot box see Run down.

Illegal pitch It is an illegal pitch if the pitcher's back foot is not in contact with the pitcher's plate, or if he pitches quickly after receiving the ball without giving the batter sufficient preparation.

ILLEGAL PITCH
In order for a pitch to be legal the pitcher's back foot must be in contact with the plate at the moment of delivery

If runners are on base after an illegal pitch is called, they are entitled to advance by one base.

Infielder A fielder who takes up a position in the infield is an infielder. The first baseman, second baseman, third baseman and shortstop are the infielders.

Infield fly An infield fly is a fly ball that can be caught readily by an infielder. The fielder must make every attempt to catch it and not deliberately drop it in an effort to force a double play. The umpire will immediately call 'infield fly' for the benefit of the runners. (For details of the full implication of an infield fly see page 47.)

In flight A ball in flight is a batted, thrown or pitched ball before it hits the ground or another object other than a fielder.

Inning An inning is when both teams have been to bat and three men have been put out. When one team has been to bat, it is called a half-inning. Each team bats for nine innings.

Interference Interference is when a player impedes another player from either fielding or batting. In some cases umpires impede players – accidentally, of course!

In the dirt A low pitch that virtually hits home plate.

Knuckleball A slow ball with an unpredictable flight is called a knuckleball. (See pitching technique on page 56.)

Line drive A ball hit hard which travels in a straight line is known as a line drive.

Live ball A live ball is a ball which is in play.

Loaded bases When all bases are occupied by runners, they are said to be loaded.

No-hitter A pitcher is said to have had a no-hitter when he has prevented the opposing batters from making a safe hit.

Obstruction Obstruction is when a fielder, not in possession of the ball and not in the process of fielding, deliberately impedes a runner. Unlike interference, obstruction is a deliberate act.

Offensive team The offensive team (often just called the 'offence') is the team at bat.

On deck The batter waiting in the on deck circle is said to be on deck.

Out(s) When one player has been put out, the offensive team is said to have had one out. Once a team has three outs, their inning comes to a close and it is the turn of the other team to bat.

Outfielder An outfielder takes up a position in the outfield.

Oversliding Oversliding is when an offensive player, sliding towards a base, overslides the base as a result of his own momentum.

Pinch hitter A substitute batter is called a pinch hitter.

Pitch The delivery of the ball from the pitcher to the batter.

Pitcher The pitcher is the person who has the responsibility for pitching the ball to the batter.

Pitcher's plate The part of the pitcher's mound on which he must have his pivoted foot at the time of pitching. The entire foot must be either on, or in front of and touching, the plate. Also known as the pitcher's rubber.

Pivot foot The pitcher's pivot foot is that foot which makes contact with the pitcher's plate at the time of delivering his pitch.

Put out On a force play, if a fielder touches a base with any part of his body while holding the ball securely in his hand or glove, he is said to have made a put out, and consequently puts out the runner heading for that base.

PUT OUT
The runner is 'put out' because the baseman has clearly collected the ball while making contact with the base, and before the runner touched the base

Quick pitch A quick pitch is a deliberate attempt by the pitcher to catch the batter unaware. Such a pitch is an illegal pitch.

Relief pitcher A pitcher who replaces the previous pitcher during a game is called the relief pitcher. A relief pitcher cannot be substi-

tuted until he has put out the first batter he pitches to, or the batter reaches first base, or the team's inning comes to a close.

Retouch A retouch is when a runner makes a legal return to a base.

Run A run is made when the runner touches first, second, third and home plate in the correct order. Also known as a score.

Run down A run down is when the defensive team traps or catches a base runner in between bases. It is often referred to as being 'caught in the hot box'.

Runner An offensive player becomes a runner once he has finished his time at bat, providing he is not out.

Runs batted in (RBI) A player is credited with runs scored as a result of his hit, whether they be by him or as a result of getting other players home. All runs are credited to his runs batted in total.

Safe If an offensive player safely reaches a base which he was attempting to reach he is said to be safe, and that is the call of the umpire to advise the fielders he has successfully made the base.

Score see Run.

Single A hit that just earns the batter a move to first base is called a single. The term does not apply in the case of a runner moving from one base to the next.

Slider One of the four basic types of pitch, the slider curves sharply sideways and down from the batter at the last minute. (See pitching technique on page 56.)

Split-fingered fastball A more recent innovation for pitchers is the split-fingered fastball. It is similar to the fastball but dips wickedly at the last moment. (See pitching technique on page 55.)

Squeeze play When a team has a player on third base they can score that runner by the batter playing a bunt.

Steal Runners do not have to wait for the pitch to be completed before setting off for the next base, they can steal a base. But most pitchers are fully aware if a runner is going to attempt a steal.

Strike A strike is a legal pitch if:
a. The batter swings at the pitch and misses.
b. The ball passes through the strike zone whether the batter attempts to hit it or not.
c. The ball is played into foul territory. However, if the batter has two strikes against him, a third strike cannot be called.
d. A bunted ball is played into foul territory.
e. The ball touches the batter as he swings at it.
f. The ball touches the batter within the strike zone.
g. The batter plays a foul tip.

Strike out A batter has struck out if he has three strikes against him.

STRIKE ZONE
The imaginary area directly above home plate and between the batter's knees and the middle of his chest, when a normal stance is taken up, is the strike zone, and pitches should pass through that area if a 'strike' is to be called

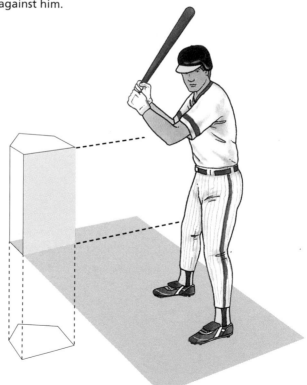

Strike zone The strike zone is the area to which the pitcher tries to deliver the ball. It covers the area over the home plate and between the top of the batter's knees and the middle of his chest when he assumes his natural stance. The umpire is responsible for assessing the strike zone and calling whether a delivery is a strike or a ball.

Switch hitter A batter who can hit from the left-hand and right-hand side of the plate is a switch hitter.

Tag A runner can be tagged by a fielder and put out, if the fielder touches the runner with the ball or with his hand or glove holding the ball.

Throw A throw is the propelling of the ball from one fielder to another. A throw must not be confused with the pitch. It is the pitcher who pitches, all other players throw.

Tie game A tie game is when both sides have the same number of runs at the end of the allotted number of innings. Extra innings are played until a winner is found.

Top of the ... 6th, 7th, etc. First half of the innings.

Triple If a batter reaches third base as a result of one hit he scores a triple.

Triple play A triple play is when the defensive team puts out three offensive players as a result of one continuous action.

Walk see Base on balls.

Wild pitch A wild pitch is one that is delivered so high, low or wide that the catcher has difficulty in catching it, and a runner advances.

TAG
A runner is tagged as a result of the fielder touching him while in possession of the ball, and before the runner reaches a base

Overleaf: Although this runner has successfully reached his base, he must get up again quickly so he is ready to sprint to the next base

The game – a guide

Baseball is played by two teams, each with nine players. Most professional teams have a squad of around twenty-five.

Rules of baseball

The game is controlled by four umpires, one positioned at each of the first three bases, and the other behind the catcher; he is the umpire-in-chief. It is his responsibility to decide whether a pitch is a ball or a strike, and to control the game in general.

The nine players, when on the defence, are as follows: catcher, pitcher, first baseman, second baseman, third baseman, shortstop, left-fielder, centre-fielder and right-fielder. The pitcher and catcher have their own specifically designated areas of the field as we have already seen but the other seven fielders can stand anywhere provided they are in fair territory. There are very few teams, however, who adopt different fielding positions from those shown.

The fascination of baseball is the battle between the pitcher and batter. The batter is trying to get on base, or to help his colleagues score, while the pitcher is doing his level best to prevent this happening.

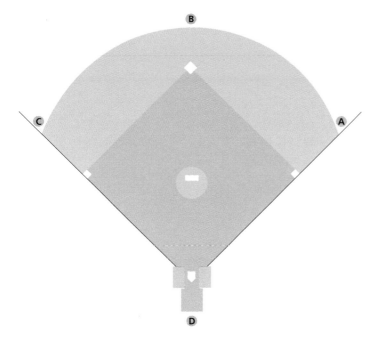

UMPIRES' POSITIONS
A: 1st base umpire
B: 2nd base umpire
C: 3rd base umpire
D: home plate umpire

The object of the game is to score more runs than your opponents. Runs are scored when runners progress round the four bases in correct order and reach the home plate.

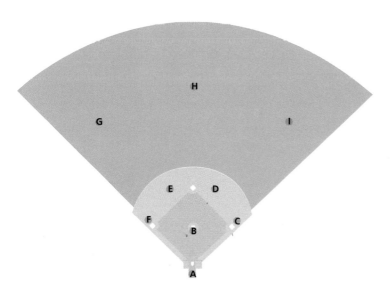

FIELDING POSITIONS
A: catcher
B: pitcher
C: 1st baseman
D: 2nd baseman
E: shortstop
F: 3rd baseman
G: left-fielder
H: centre-fielder
I: right-fielder

Runs do not have to be scored as a result of one hit, known as a home run, but runners can progress one base at a time before heading for the home plate.

It all sounds easy doesn't it? Don't be fooled …

The strategically placed fielders are fully aware of runners' positions and their quick reflexes can result in two, or occasionally three, players being put out before they reach their next base, as a result of one continuous play.

Down to basics

Each team has nine innings. A team's inning lasts until three men have been put out. Teams take it in turn to bat (offence) and field (defence). If both teams have scored the same number of runs at the end of nine innings, extra full innings are played until a winner is found. The visiting team is always the first to bat.

Play commences when the first batter has taken up position in the batter's box and the plate umpire calls 'play'. From that moment the ball is live and in play.

Players of the batting side take it in strict rotation to bat and, if a player is substituted, his replacement takes his place in the batting order. If a player is put out he retains his place in the order and when, or if, his turn comes up again, either in the same or subsequent innings, he can go to bat again.

Runs are scored, as we have said before, by circling all bases and reaching home plate without being put out. A batter can be out in a variety of ways, the most frequent being when he hits a ball into the air (a fly ball) and it is caught by a fielder, whether it is hit into fair or foul territory. Other common ways of being out include when the batter hits an infield fly or when he has three strikes against him. A runner is out if he is tagged by a fielder in between bases, or the base to which he is running is tagged by the fielder on a force play.

The easiest way to score a run is by hitting a homer (a home run). I say easiest only because it does not involve the tactical battle needed to progress from base to base. If you hit a homer, you can run, or even stroll, around the bases without being put out. Furthermore, players on bases in front of you all score runs automatically, though they must still make contact with all bases in the correct sequence on the way to the home plate.

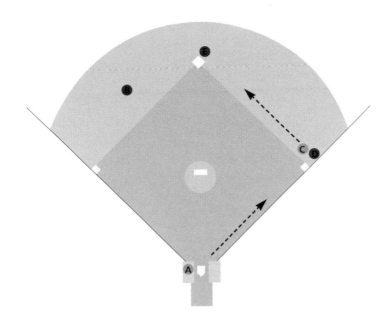

DOUBLE
If batter A hits to shortstop B then A has to run to first base, thus forcing runner C off the base. B throws to second baseman E, who touches the base and puts out C. E then throws to D (first baseman), who puts out A. This is the most common of the many double plays which can occur in baseball

Don't get the impression that most runs are scored this way; they are not. When you stand there and face a pitch from the pitcher, you will see just how hard it is even to make contact with the ball, let alone hit it out of the ground for a home run!

Most runs are scored by batters making a hit which takes them to first or second base, which in turn sends any runners on bases in front of him on by one or more bases until, hopefully, one of them reaches home plate.

The essence of the game is that intriguing battle between pitcher and batter. The pitcher must pitch the ball into the strike zone. If he does not, and the batter does not swing at it, the home plate umpire will call it a 'ball'. A pitch that does enter the strike zone is called a 'strike' (there are other rules and restrictions governing balls and strikes: see definition on page 34). A batter is allowed two strikes only against him. If he has a third he is automatically out. However, the pitcher is allowed to deliver only three balls. If he pitches a fourth then the batter automatically walks to first base. With the bases loaded, the runner on third base would, in this case, automatically score a run. So, if you are pitching and there are runners on first base, first and second base or first, second and third base, they all advance automatically.

If the batter successfully hits the ball into fair territory he must drop his bat and run to first base, or beyond it if it is safe to do so. He must arrive at the base before the ball is retrieved and thrown to the first baseman. If the first baseman catches the ball and makes contact with the base before the batter (who has now become a runner) gets there, then the runner is out. If the batter safely proceeds past first base, then a fielder must tag him before he reaches another base safely to make an out.

Runners on bases do not have to wait for the pitch before they run to the next base – they can 'steal' a base. But pitchers and catchers are well aware when a steal is being attempted and such a move is often thwarted by quick thinking. Stealing is not as simple as it sounds and is quite an art. Some players in Major League baseball are specialists at stealing bases.

If a batter is out as a result of a fly ball being caught, all runners who advanced during the hit must return to their previous base. However, a runner can advance to the next base provided he holds on to his base until after the catch has been made, but there is then a great risk of being tagged out.

The umpires

The umpires are the sole arbitrators of events on the field, and are responsible for seeing that players act in a disciplined manner and according to the rules. Players cannot dispute the home plate umpire's decision regarding balls and strikes but can make appeals over other matters.

The most important umpire is the home plate umpire (known as the umpire-in-chief). His duties, in addition to calling balls and strikes, include keeping a note of team changes and responsibility for replacing damaged balls. As his name implies, he is also respon-sible for any action around the home plate.

The other umpires can take any position on the field that provides them with a clear view and the ability to make decisions relating to each of the bases for which they are responsible.

The first base umpire, by definition, guards the first base. He is responsible for checking that runners reach base properly, or if a successful tag is made. He also keeps an eye on right-handed batters to check whether they make full- or half-swings at the ball, which assists the home plate umpire in deciding whether to call a

UMPIRES' SIGNALS

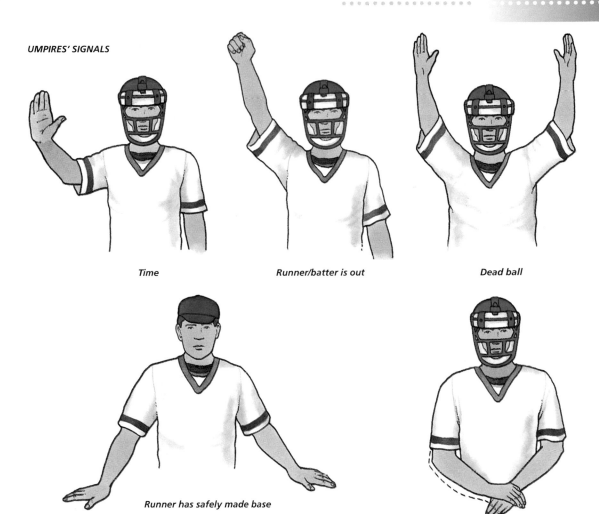

Time   Runner/batter is out   Dead ball

Runner has safely made base

ball or strike. The first base umpire, like all umpires, has to see that players do not obstruct one another and make sure all runners keep within 3ft (0.91m) of the lines when running between bases.

The second base umpire stands between second and third base and the third base umpire stands 8–10ft (2.5–3m) behind third base. Like the first base umpire he has to judge whether a batter (left-handed in this case) has made a full- or half-swing at the ball.

Umpires make signals to indicate to the crowd what is happening, yet strangely the rules of baseball make no provision for a standardized set of signals. Most umpires, however, have adopted a universally accepted set of their own.

Foul tip. (Home plate umpire makes striking movement on back of left hand with palm of his right hand)

Summary: The object of the game for the offensive side is to get players around the bases until one, or as many as possible, reach home plate to score a run. The defensive side tries to stop them making runs by putting players out before they get round the bases. Each team has nine innings and the team with the most runs at the end of the nine is the winner. Extra innings are played if both teams are level. If the team batting second is in the lead after 8½ innings, they do not need to bat again.

These then are the simplified rules of baseball. However, the game is more complex than that and hopefully the Rules Clinic on the following pages will clear up some of the more intricate problems you may come up against either playing or watching this fascinating sport.

LINE SCORES

Game 1:

	1	2	3	4	5	6	7	8	9	TOTAL
Detroit	0	0	1	0	0	1	1	2	0	5
Minnesota	0	1	0	0	3	0	0	4	X	8

Minnesota won 8–5 and led series 1–0

Game 2:

	1	2	3	4	5	6	7	8	9	TOTAL
Detroit	0	2	0	0	0	0	0	1	0	3
Minnesota	0	3	0	2	1	0	0	0	X	6

Minnesota won 6–3 and led series 2–0

Game 3:

	1	2	3	4	5	6	7	8	9	TOTAL
Minnesota	0	0	0	2	0	2	2	0	0	6
Detroit	0	0	5	0	0	0	0	2	X	7

Detroit won 7–6, but trailed series 1–2

Game 4:

	1	2	3	4	5	6	7	8	9	TOTAL
Minnesota	0	0	1	1	1	1	0	1	0	5
Detroit	1	0	0	0	1	1	0	0	0	3

Minnesota won 5–3 and led series 3–1

Game 5:

	1	2	3	4	5	6	7	8	9	TOTAL
Minnesota	0	4	0	0	0	0	1	1	3	9
Detroit	0	0	0	3	0	0	0	1	1	5

Minnesota won 9–5 and won series 4–1

Reproduced left are the line scores from the best-of-seven game eliminator to see which team would represent the AL in the 1987 World Series. The most runs scored in one inning was 5 by Detroit, in the bottom of the 3rd in game 3. The 'X' in the bottom of the 9th in games 1, 2 and 3 means the team batting second had already won and did not need to bat again

The most important man in the game: the pitcher

Rules clinic

This chapter offers a unique, question-and-answer guide to many commonly asked queries about baseball.

I understand about 'balls' and 'strikes', but what would happen if a pitch hits the ground and then passes through the strike zone; would that be a ball or a strike?
It would be a ball. If such a delivery hit the batter then he would be entitled to an automatic walk to first base.

Can a catch be made with the player over a boundary line or fence?
Yes. If, however, a player makes a catch and then drops the ball as a result of running into a boundary fence it is not a catch.

Does the same player start each new inning at bat for his team?
No, the batting order is in strict rotation. If player no 7 was the last man at bat in the previous inning then no 8 starts the batting when his team next goes to bat.

If a batter is on two strikes and he hits into foul territory, is he out?
No. Normally balls hit into foul territory are called 'strikes', but if a batter has two strikes against him a ball hit foul will not be called a third strike. However, if the batter plays a bunt which goes into foul territory it is called a 'strike'.

Does the batter have to stand with both feet in the batter's box, or does he just need to have one foot in?
He must have both feet in the box. If he hits a ball while one or both feet are outside the box he will be given out.

I have sometimes seen a batter have three strikes against him but still become a runner. How can this happen?
If the catcher fails to catch the ball after a third strike the batter is not out and becomes a runner, but only if: (a) the first base is unoccupied or (b) the first base is occupied with two men out.

Can a batter or runner deliberately cause interference with a fielder in order to help advance his own players?
No. And if a player is ruled out for interference, all runners must return to the last base they legally touched before the interference.

Please clarify the infield fly rule. Why is it a player cannot deliberately not make the catch?
Firstly, a batter who hits a ball that the umpire calls an infield fly is automatically out if the ball is fair, whether it is caught or not. The rule applies only when first and second or first, second and third bases are occupied, with less than two outs, and the ball could be caught by an infielder without difficulty.

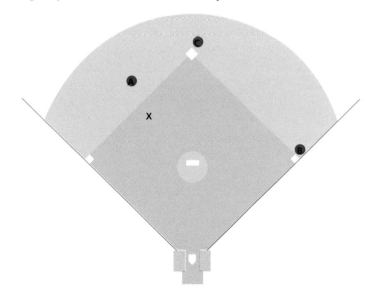

INFIELD FLY
The batter hits the ball to position X. The home plate umpire calls it an infield fly because it can be easily caught, probably by shortstop A, and the batting side has runners B and C on the first two bases. As we saw earlier, (a) a batter is out if caught, and (b) a runner cannot run until the ball is caught. In the case of the infield fly, if caught the batter is out, and runners B and C can stay safely on their bases. If shortstop A deliberately or otherwise drops the catch, the batter would have to run to first base, which would then force B and C off base. By virtue of his position on the field shortstop A could possibly put out two, or even three, men, and thus gain an unfair advantage by not making the catch. The infield fly rule, therefore, states that the batter is out if the ball is fair whether the ball is caught or not. Runners B and C don't then have to leave their bases

Are all balls hit out of the playing field home runs?
No. If the ball passes over the boundary fence at a distance of at least 250ft (76m) from the home plate then it is a home run and the batter is entitled to complete a circuit of the bases without risk of being put out. But if he hits a fair fly ball out of the field at a point less than 250ft (76m) from home plate then he is entitled only to walk to second base. Before each game, the manager or coach of the home team advises the umpire-in-chief and the opposing manager or coach of special ground rules relating to the playing field.

Is a ball hit into the crowd used again?
No, not in Major League baseball, but in the amateur game balls are quite often used until they are virtually unplayable.

Does the batter have to hit a pitch?
No, but once he does, and the ball goes into fair territory, he must drop his bat and run.

When is the ball dead?
When the home plate umpire calls 'time', which may be for a variety of reasons. The ball may be damaged, he may have seen an infringement, weather conditions may make it necessary, or a manager/coach may have called for a 'time-out'. Once the ball is dead the batting side may not run, score runs or be put out. Also the ball is dead when it hits a batter or runner, or is touched by a fan while in play.

Can a substituted player return to the game at a later stage?
No, once he is taken out of the game that is it, he stays out.

What happens if a pitch hits the batter?
The batter will also be entitled to walk to first base and all runners, if forced, will advance one base. The exceptions are when a batter is hit in the strike zone, in which case a strike will be called, or the batter does not make a reasonable effort to avoid the pitch.

Is a runner allowed to vary more than 3ft (0.91m) from the direct line between bases?
No, unless he has to avoid a fielder attempting to recover the ball. In this case he may run round him and outside the 3ft (0.91m) line.

What happens if a base is accidentally moved from its original position?
The runner should aim towards the original position of the base, rather than its new position, if it is unreasonably out of position. A runner cannot be out by a baseman tagging the base when at its new position.

What is the ruling if a balk is called?
If there are runners on base, each advances one base. If there are no runners on base a 'ball' is called.

If a side has two men out and the runner on third base reaches home but the batter is put out before he reaches first base, would the run score?
No. Likewise if a runner reached home and a runner behind him incorrectly touched a base he would be out and the run not count.

If a fly ball lands in fair territory and then bounces into foul territory is it a fair or foul ball?
If it lands on the infield between home and first base, or home and third base, and then goes into foul territory before first or third base without hitting a fielder or umpire, then it is a foul ball. If it first lands on or beyond first or third base in fair territory, and then goes into foul territory, it is a fair hit.

You have said earlier that a pitcher must stand facing the base he is throwing to; what if he doesn't?
He will be penalized by the umpire calling a balk. In every case the pitcher must step directly towards the base to which he is throwing.

I know a player cannot use his cap, or other pieces of clothing or equipment, to field a ball, but is it still a penalty if a fielder throws his cap at a ball and misses?
Perhaps surprisingly, no.

Can a runner intentionally kick or interfere with a batted or thrown ball so as to hinder the fielder?
No. If he does he is out.

FAIR/FOUL BALLS
Ball A is a foul ball, ball B is fair

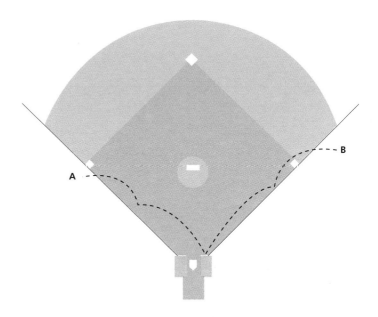

Can a runner overtake another runner?
Only if the runner in front is out, otherwise you cannot go past another runner.

If I drop my bat and the ball rolls against it, is it a penalty?
If in the opinion of the umpire the bat drop was unintentional and it did not interfere with the course of the ball, then the ball is live and in fair play.

Why don't you see pitchers shining the ball by rubbing it on their trousers like bowlers in cricket?
Because they are not allowed to. They are not allowed to deface the ball in any way, and that includes rubbing it on their clothing. They should not do anything to it that is likely to affect its true flight. For any violation the umpire will call a 'ball' and for subsequent offences the pitcher is likely to be removed from the game.

Is a relief pitcher allowed some warm-up throws?
Yes, even though he will have been pitching regularly in the 'bullpen' before coming on. Once he arrives at the mound he is allowed a maximum of eight practice pitches to his catcher.

Common sense tells me the pitcher should not pitch directly at the batter, but what if he does?

The umpire will warn the pitcher and his team manager that any future violation will result in his being removed from the field. If a pitched ball hits the batter he is entitled to walk to first base. If he is hit while making no attempt at the ball and makes no effort to get out of the way then it is only a ball. However, if the batter is hit in the strike zone then that is his fault for being there and a strike is called.

If a runner or runners advance bases after a hit which subsequently goes foul, can they hold their base or do they have to return?

The ball is dead and consequently they cannot run. They have to return, but cannot be put out.

What happens to runners who have left their base when a fly ball is caught?

They have to return to their original base, thereby incurring the risk of being tagged. Therefore if the fielding team tag the base before a runner returns, the runner is out. They cannot run until the ball has been caught. Rarely will you see leading professionals leave their base when a fly ball has been hit because there is little risk of it being dropped.

If a runner is attempting a 'steal' but decides against it, does he or the base have to be tagged in order for him to be put out?

The runner.

If a runner is off his base and a batted ball hits the base, is the runner out?

No. He can be out only if the base is tagged by a fielder.

Why does the pitcher sometimes deliberately pitch four balls without making any effort to obtain strikes or allowing the batter the chance of a hit?

It is a tactical play. A team manager will, on seeing which of the opposing team is next to bat, instruct his pitcher to take this action. The manager may feel it better to let the batter walk to first base than risk his making a successful hit.

Overleaf: To claim a base, the runner must make contact with it with any part of his body before the baseman tags the base or the runner is tagged while running between bases

Technique

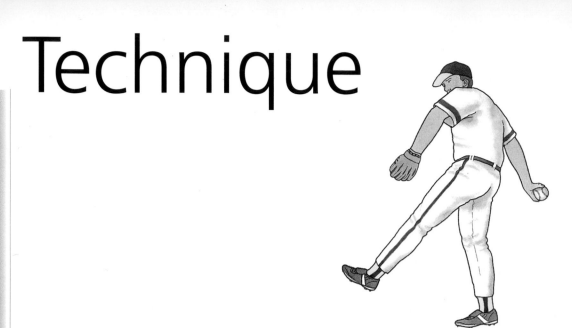

Baseball is all about gaining expertise in one or more of the skills of pitching, batting, running, fielding and catching. Each is a specialized activity in its own right, and we will highlight how best to tackle each.

PITCHING

As we have said earlier, the essence of a game of baseball is the battle between the pitcher and batter. A good pitcher will always outplay a good batter, but a good batter will destroy a poor pitcher. The pitcher undoubtedly has a major influence on the game.

A top-quality pitcher pitches the ball at around 90mph (145km/h), and on average five times to each batter. This puts excessive strain on the arm and shoulder. Good pitchers reckon they need four days' rest in between matches, and after each game they immediately place ice bags on their arms for twenty minutes or so.

The pitcher's role is to deceive the batter with a collection of swerving and dipping pitches in an effort to get him out. As part of his deception the pitcher is capable of delivering a variety of different pitches, each of which moves in the air in a different way.

Unlike cricket, where most of the ball action occurs after it has hit the pitch, in baseball all the ball movement is in the air. Pitchers rely on their catchers to assist them with advice about what type of pitch to make, even though the ultimate choice is with the pitcher.

There are several basic types of pitch, and those most commonly used by leading players are as follows.

Fastball

The ball is held with the thumb underneath and the first two fingers on top of the ball, and held close together. The ball is pitched at speed in a straight line from the pitcher's mound directly towards the home plate. Because the mound is elevated the ball travels downwards towards the plate. If it is hit by the batter the ball will most probably be hit along the ground, or low.

FASTBALL

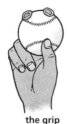

the grip

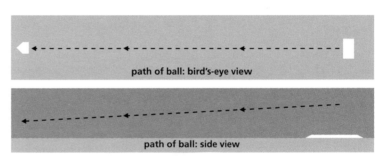

path of ball: bird's-eye view

path of ball: side view

Split-fingered fastball

A relatively new type of pitch. It is similar to the conventional fastball but the two fingers on top of the ball are spread apart. The result is that the ball travels in a straight line towards the home plate but dips sharply towards the end of its flight. Difficult to distinguish from an ordinary fastball.

SPLIT-FINGERED FASTBALL

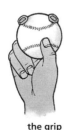

the grip

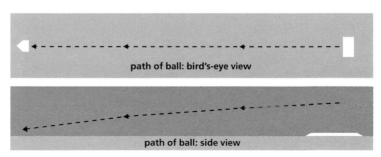

path of ball: bird's-eye view

path of ball: side view

Curveball

The grip is the same as the fastball but the fingers are parallel to the seam. At the moment of delivery the pitcher twists his wrist, with the effect that the ball not only travels towards the home plate from right to left (the opposite for a left-handed pitcher), but it also dips at the last minute.

CURVEBALL
Like the fastball, the curveball also dips towards home plate

the grip

path of ball: bird's-eye view from right-handed pitcher

Slider

The ball is gripped similarly to the curveball but tighter. The ball appears to be a fastball to the batter but it fades away, as well as dipping, from the plate at the last minute. A difficult pitch to identify.

SLIDER
The grip for the slider is a tighter version of that for the curveball

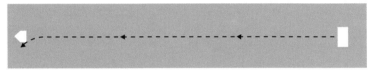

path of ball: bird's-eye view from right-handed pitcher

Knuckleball

The knuckleball is held between the thumb and the first joints on two or three fingers. Because it is held like this the ball does not actually spin in flight. It does however turn, but that is as a result of the air currents picking up the seams of the ball. It has to be delivered slowly otherwise there would be no movement of the ball and it would be easy to hit. The knuckleball is difficult to perfect, but is very effective if pitched properly.

KNUCKLEBALL

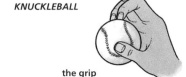

the grip

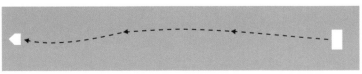

path of ball: bird's-eye view

Screwball

The screwball is the opposite of a curveball. The ball curves from the left to the right when delivered by a right-handed pitcher (the opposite for a left-handed pitcher). To deliver a screwball a right-handed pitcher will move so the palm of his hand is facing third base during delivery.

SCREWBALL

path of ball: bird's-eye view from right-handed pitcher

Change up

To deliver a slower ball (known as a change up) the ball is held more towards the palm of the hand but with the finger positions as shown on the right.

CHANGE UP

the grip

Pitcher's action

All pitchers hold the ball differently, and only experience will tell you the best way to get the desired results of the basic pitches.

When starting his pitch, the pitcher stands facing the batter. He then raises his hands above his head, keeping the ball in his glove and hidden from the batter. The back foot must remain on the plate and as he brings his other leg upwards, as part of his wind-up, the back foot pivots. He then turns towards the batter, the front leg comes forward, and the delivery is completed. With the follow-through and shape of the mound the front foot is carried forward and the pitcher is carried by his momentum towards the batter. At the moment of delivery, for maximum effect, the delivering arm should be parallel with the floor. It is best to pitch towards the bottom of the strike zone because that way, if the ball is hit, there is less chance of its being hit for a home run.

A batter will always be able to tell what kind of delivery the pitcher will make by looking at his grip of the ball. That is why the pitcher has a heavily webbed glove to hide his grip from the batter and thus put the initiative in the pitcher's favour. The pitcher must be ready to try and outwit the batter by constantly varying his pitches. On the other hand, if you pitched, say, three successive fastballs, you could just as easily confuse the batter because he would be expecting you to vary your pitches. The battle between pitcher and batter can therefore be described as 'chess with a bat and ball' ...

PITCHER'S ACTION
The wind-up ...

... After delivery, see how the pitcher's follow-through makes his body parallel to the ground

If we look at the pitcher's 'wind-up' it will be seen in the fourth diagram that the batter gets a glimpse of the pitcher's grip on the ball. This is the first indication the batter will get as to the type of pitch. From that he has to try and assess what kind of pitch to expect.

'HIDING' THE BALL FROM THE BATTER
To prevent the batter getting a glimpse of the grip, the pitcher 'hides' the ball in his glove

BATTING

Why can't a batter always hit the ball? Well, you ought to know the answer to that after reading the previous pages about the pitcher. The pitcher has the advantage over the batter of knowing how the ball is going to be pitched. Furthermore, the ball comes towards the batter at speeds of 90–95mph (145–155 km/h) and the batter has about one-eleventh of a second to decide what kind of pitch it is, whether to attempt to hit it, or whether to leave it in the hope of its being called a ball. Anticipation is therefore the key to becoming a successful batter.

Most batters adopt a basic stance with the weight on their back foot. A couple of practice swings are customary between pitches to keep the arms 'loosened up'. The bat should be held firmly but not gripped too tight. Timing is all-important, and when making contact with the ball, bat and ball should be about 18in (45cm) in front of the body.

It is important to keep your eye on the ball at all times, and make up your mind as late as possible what kind of pitch it is. Once you have decided you are going to hit the ball, your weight should shift to your front foot as you bring the bat down ready for the hit.

Hitting the ball into foul territory often happens for two reasons: by hitting the ball too early, or by hitting it too late. For a right-handed batter, if hit too early the ball will generally go into the left foul territory and if too late into the right foul territory.

Because the initiative is with the pitcher, it is not always possible to hit the ball to the part of the field you want to, let alone hit it at all! If a runner is on third base and there is a chance of a run, you should attempt to hit the ball safely into the right side of the field. Alternatively, if there is no player on third base then you would be better to hit the ball to the left side to enable you to get to first base. In both cases you are giving the fielder the maximum amount of throwing distance to try and put out the appropriate runner.

BATTING

This is the standard stance adopted by batters (above left). Note where the ball is when hit, together with the complete follow-through ...

... As you bring the bat down you should begin to transfer your weight to your front foot

One of the skills of batting is bunting. The normal stance is adopted but, once the ball is pitched, you slide your top hand down the bat and, rather than swinging at the ball, hold the bat in front of the ball to 'deaden' the pitch. The ball is aimed towards first or third base and will travel about 20–25ft (6–8m). The idea of the bunt is to catch the baseman, catcher or pitcher off guard. By the time they have decided who will retrieve the ball you will either have made first base yourself or another runner could have got home, which is generally the purpose of a bunt.

RUNNING

Once you have made a fair hit you must drop the bat and run. From that moment you become a runner and your task is then to get round all the bases in the correct order, touching each in turn, before getting to home plate for a run.

Speed is the key to successful running, but you must also be aware of where your team-mates are. There is no point in running from second to third base if you are putting a colleague on third base in jeopardy when there was no need for you to run in the first place. If you were forced to run, of course that is a different matter.

To claim a base legally you must make contact with it with any part of your body before the baseman tags the base, or before you are tagged while running between bases. To tag you the fielder has to make contact with you while he is holding the ball … he cannot throw the ball at you.

You must always keep a careful watch on what decision umpires make about colleagues ahead of you on other bases. If a player is given out then the base is free for you to run at, but if he is not out and stays on base then you cannot take his base. Always being aware of what is happening around you is the key to successful running.

Don't forget that if a batter hits a fly ball that is caught legally you have to return to your base, at the risk of being put out if you don't. You will not see good players start their run after a fly ball until it has been caught.

Stealing bases is a legitimate part of

BUNTING
When bunting, the top hand is moved from its normal position A, and placed further down the bat at B. (The batter here is left-handed)

RUNNER VERSUS BASEMAN
The battle for base: the intriguing conflict between runner and baseman. Such close situations call for good umpiring

RUNNING BETWEEN BASES
Base runners should always be
ready to advance
to the next
base ...

running, but is an art. The pitcher has the advantage when you are trying to steal, but careful timing can often result in a successful steal. All runners should, at the moment of the pitch, stand a few yards from the base, ready to start the run to the next base, but not too far away to return quickly in case the pitcher tries to put him out. As the rules state that a pitcher must point his foot towards the base when going for a put out on a steal, you should keep a watch on the pitcher's feet; that is the clue to whether he is going for the pitch or trying to put somebody out who is contemplating a steal. Beware, though; good pitchers can fool runners into thinking they are going to pitch, then suddenly turn and throw to a baseman for a put out.

FIELDING AND CATCHING

Fielders are divided into two categories: infielders, such as first baseman and shortstop, and outfielders. All fielders need to be fit, be able to catch the ball, throw it accurately and over great distances, and more important, be alert and aware of what play is taking place around the diamond.

Fielders are, as we know, allowed to wear a glove to aid them, but one important rule to remember concerning the glove is: when collecting high balls, the fingers of the glove point upwards; when

collecting low balls, the fingers of the glove point downwards. The ball is gathered in the glove and then thrown with the ungloved hand. Don't forget, the glove is worn on the 'wrong' hand, if you are right-handed, it is worn on the left hand.

We have seen earlier what positions fielders take, but let us look closely at what each of them does specifically.

... If they have to slide into a base they should get up quickly in case they have to move on to the next base

First baseman The first baseman plays an important role. Because so many balls are thrown to him in order to get out a batter/runner at his base (he has more balls thrown to him than any other baseman), he is allowed to wear a bigger glove. It is more advantageous for the first baseman to be left-handed because after collecting the ball he does not have to shift his body position to throw to any other bases.

Second baseman The second baseman will stand near to his base but more towards first base than third because the shortstop can cover the area between second and third. Most double plays involve the second baseman. Rarely are second basemen left-handed.

Third baseman The least-used of all basemen, he still has to be alert like his colleagues. Because he throws the ball either ahead of him or to his left, it pays for a third baseman to be right-handed.

DOUBLE PLAY
In this double play the batter hits to left infield, forcing the runner off first base. Shortstop A fields and throws to second baseman B, who puts out the runner then throws to the first baseman C, who puts out the batter

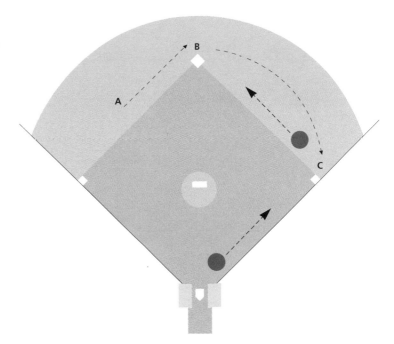

Shortstop The most active of the infielders, the shortstop is responsible for retrieving a large number of balls and for tagging out runners and accurately throwing to the appropriate baseman. As double plays are a vital part of a fielding side's repertoire, quick throwing and catching between basemen is important and for practice it is worth throwing balls between pitcher, catcher and the other infielders. This practice can either be in a pre-determined order, or at random, which is preferable because in a live situation you would not have much time to make your choice of throw.

Outfielders Speed at collecting balls and returning to a baseman are the main ingredient for a good outfielder. Often you see spectacular dives to stop drives but these, while looking impressive, can prove expensive. While you are lying on the ground players can be getting around bases. Outfielders must also be fearless and expect to go crashing into boundary fences, stands, etc., in an effort to retrieve hard-hit fly balls. The outfield positions are left-fielder, centre-fielder and right-fielder.

fastball

curveball

slider

change up

CATCHER'S SIGNALS
The catcher assists the pitcher by suggesting which pitch to deliver. The batter cannot see the signals, but men on the second or third bases can, and will, in turn try to pass the information on to the batter

Catcher The catcher plays a very important role in any team. He is the player who has a clear view of all the action and consequently passes on information to his team-mates. The liaison between catcher and pitcher is very important. The catcher studies batters and advises pitchers what sort of pitch to make and where to make it to.

Overleaf: All the excitement and timing of professional baseball is captured in this action shot of George Williams of the Oakland A's attempting to reach base while being challenged by Ray Durham of the White Sox

History & development of softball

Softball is a smaller but faster variation of baseball. It is a popular sport, because it does not require as much space as baseball.

Unlike baseball, softball can trace its exact roots. In 1887, George Hancock, of the Farragut Boat Club of Illinois, Chicago saw the dramatic growth of baseball and thought it would be even more popular if it could be played indoors. To do that, however, the game had to be scaled down, and Hancock drew up a set of rules for a smaller version of baseball. Naturally the new game was called 'Indoor Baseball'. (Hancock's imagination only stretched so far!) The new game became popular in its own right and moved outdoors. Lewis Rober of the Minneapolis Fire Department fixed the first definite rules of softball and called his game 'Kitten Ball'. It was later re-named 'Mush Ball' before Walter Hakanson named it 'Softball' in 1926. The game became very popular during the depression of the 1930s and after a national softball tournament at the Chicago World Fair in 1933 the first set of standardized rules was drawn up. The same year the Amateur Softball Association of America was formed, and their first championships held.

In the early 1950s softball became one of the biggest participation sports in the United States and it became a truly international sport following the formation of the International Softball Federation in 1950. By 1965 the game was played in more than fifty countries. The first world championships for women were held at Melbourne, Australia in 1965 and the following year the first men's world championships were held. Today, the rules of softball are printed in more than a dozen languages, highlighting the international appeal of the game.

Part of the success of softball is its appeal to women and the fact that many teams are mixed.

Equipment

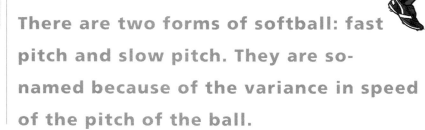

There are two forms of softball: fast pitch and slow pitch. They are so-named because of the variance in speed of the pitch of the ball.

In slow pitch, the ball must be pitched in an arc from the pitcher to the batter and not unreasonably fast. In fast pitch, however, the ball – providing it is delivered legally – can be pitched as fast as the pitcher likes.

There are many fundamental differences between softball and baseball. The playing area is smaller; the ball is bigger; a game lasts only seven innings; the pitcher throws from a shorter distance; all pitches are underarm; and, an important point, the pitcher must show the ball to the batter at all times. Protective clothing is the same as in baseball but bats are smaller.

The principal differences between baseball and softball are as follows.

The pitch

The shape of the playing area is the same in both games but the measurements differ. The distances between bases vary depending upon which variety of softball is played and whether by men or women. There are also slight variations for boys and girls under fifteen. The most common measurements are as follows:

Fast pitch – male   60ft (18.29m)
Fast pitch – female   60ft (18.29m)
Slow pitch – male 65ft (19.81m)
Slow pitch – female   60ft (18.29m)

The distance between the pitcher's plate and home plate also varies according to which form of softball you play. The distances are:

Fast pitch – male   46ft (14.02m)
Fast pitch – female   40ft (12.19m)
Slow pitch – male 46ft (14.02m)
Slow pitch – female   46ft (14.02m)

The layout of the field is the same as for baseball, with infield and outfield, and fair and foul territories (see page 17).

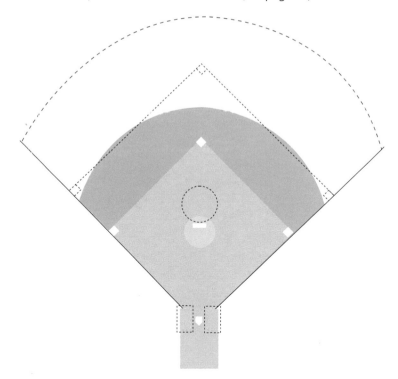

THE INFIELD
Drawn to scale, it can clearly be seen how much smaller the infield of a standard male fast pitch softball field is compared to that of the standard baseball field. (The dotted lines denote a standard baseball field)

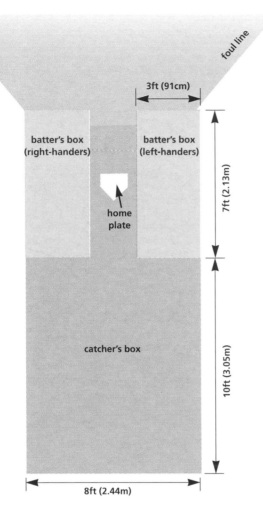

Detail of the home plate, batter's boxes and catcher's box

3ft (91cm)

batter's box
(right-handers)

batter's box
(left-handers)

home
plate

7ft (2.13m)

catcher's box

10ft (3.05m)

8ft (2.44m)

The batter's box, at 3ft by 7ft (0.91m by 2.13m), is smaller than in baseball, but the catcher's box at 8ft by 10ft (2.44m by 3.05m) is considerably bigger. The pitcher's circle, however, is slightly smaller with an 8ft (2.44m) radius. The pitcher's plate is the same size as in baseball.

The ball

The ball is bigger and heavier in softball than in baseball. It has a circumference of 11⅞–12⅛in (30.16–30.8cm) and should weigh 6¼–7oz (177.2–198.5g).

The bat

The softball bat is shorter than its baseball counterpart. It is no longer than 34in (86.36cm) with a maximum diameter of 2¼in (5.72cm) at its thickest part. The maximum weight is 38oz (1.07kg) and the safety grip should not extend further than 15in (38.1cm) down the handle.

Clothing

Fielders, pitchers and catchers all wear gloves as in baseball, and the catcher wears similar protective clothing to his baseball opposite number. Rules governing shoe cleats are however much stricter in softball.

Note. Softball terminology is much the same as in baseball, and has therefore not had a separate section devoted to it. See baseball terminology on pages 24–35.

Rules

We ought to make it clear that softball is perhaps the most incorrectly named of all sports.

It is not played with a soft ball. Far from it; the ball is bigger and heavier than a normal baseball – if you have ever been hit with a softball you will know what I mean!

Another thing that should be remembered is that there are two forms of softball: slow pitch and fast pitch. With the first variety the ball is pitched underarm in an arc. In the fast pitch variation (the more popular form of softball in Europe), the ball is delivered underarm, and as fast as the pitcher can deliver it.

The fast pitch game is a faster game than baseball and is action-packed. The slow pitch game is played in a more leisurely fashion, often by mixed teams.

The rules governing balls, strikes, tagging and running are the same as in baseball and the principle is the same ... to hit the ball and score more runs than the opposing team.

Stealing is not permitted in the slow pitch game. A runner cannot leave his base until the ball passes over home plate. Any runner who does leave his base before then is out.

Unlike baseball, a toss of a coin decides which team bats first

slow pitch
softball
strike zone

home plate

in softball. Both teams have seven innings (nine in baseball). A fast pitch team consists of nine players but a slow pitch team has ten; an extra shortstop (known as a shortfielder) is added.

As we have seen, pitching is the main difference between softball and baseball. The pitcher, apart from delivering underarm, must show the ball to the batter at all times. He cannot hide it in his glove or behind his back. Unlike baseball, therefore, the batter has the advantage over the pitcher.

The strike zone in fast pitch is the same as in baseball, that is between the batter's armpit and the top of his knees when he adopts his normal stance. In slow pitch, however, it is between the top of his knees and his higher shoulder. Balls and strikes are called in exactly the same way as in baseball.

Technique

The main difference in technique between softball and baseball is the pitching. Pitching techniques are also different for fast and slow pitch softball.

It is still possible to pitch curveballs, knuckleballs and so on, even though you are delivering underarm. Why not experiment with your own technique to find out how much you can get the ball to turn in flight with a twist of the wrist or fingers at the moment of delivery. You do not have to pitch conventional curveballs, etc., you can adopt your own pitch. As long as it fools the pitcher then it is a successful pitch.

Before starting to pitch you must stand with both feet on or touching the pitcher's plate and with your body square and your shoulders pointing to first and third bases. You must face the batter and for a period of not less than one second or more than ten seconds hold the ball in front of you with two hands. The pitch commences when one hand is taken off the ball. From then on the ball must be in full view of the batter.

One forward step towards the batter is allowed at the time of delivery. The release of the ball and follow-through must be forward and past the straight line of the body. At the moment of release, the ball must be below the hip and the wrist and no further

forward than the elbow.

Before pitching you may 'wind-up' your arm (known as the 'windmill pitch') but by only one revolution of your arm.

You are not allowed to roll the ball along the ground to deliberately prevent the batter hitting it.

In slow pitch the ball has to be pitched in an arc with its highest point 6–12ft (1.83–3.66m) from the ground. The ball must be pitched with 'moderate speed'. Any pitcher delivering balls too fast is liable to be sent off the field.

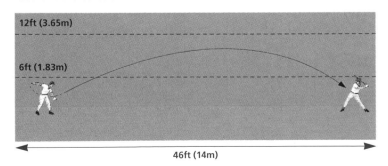

12ft (3.65m)

6ft (1.83m)

46ft (14m)

PITCHING (SLOW PITCH)
When pitching in the slow pitch game, the ball must travel in an arc. The top of the arc must be 6–12ft (1.83–3.66m) from the ground

Useful

addresses

All-American Amateur Baseball Association
331 Parkway Drive
Zanesville
OH 43701, USA

Baseball, Softball Federation of Russia
Luzhnetskaya Emb. 8
Moscow GSP 119871
Russia

British Baseball Federation
PO Box 45
Hessle HU13 0YQ

Danish Baseball Softball Federation
Junkerensvej 3
9240 Soenderholm–NIBE
Denmark

Deutscher Baseball Softball Verband
Feldbergstrasse 20–22
55118 Mainz
Germany

Federation Francaise Baseball Softball Cricket
41 rue de Fecand
75012 Paris
France

Federazione Italiana Baseball Softball
Viale Tiziano 74
00196 Roma
Italy

International Baseball Association
Avenue de Mon-Repas 24
Case Postale 131
1000 Lausanne 5
Switzerland

Irish Baseball and Softball Association
14 Innishmaan Road
Whitehall
Dublin 9
Ireland

Israel Association of Baseball
Box 109
Moshav Zofit 44925
Israel

Koninklijke Belgische Baseball en Softball Federatie
Postbus 13
2000 Antwerpen
Belgium

Koninklijke Nederlandse Baseball en Softball Bond
PO Box 60
2080 Ab Santpoort-Zuid
Nederland

Major League Baseball International
Suite 3, West Hill House
6 Swain's Lane
London N6 6QS

Major League Baseball National League/American League
350 Park Avenue
New York
NY 10022, USA

Norwegian Soft-Baseball Federation
Hauger Skolevei 1
1351 Rud, Norway

Osterreichischer Baseball Softball Verband
Stanislausgasse 2/6
1030 Wien, Austria

Polski Zwiazek Baseballu i Softballu
ul.Sygnaly 62
44–251 Rybnik Gotartowice
Poland

Real Federacion Espanola Beisbol Sofbol
Coslada 10,4 izqda
28028 Madrid, Spain

Svenska Baseboll och Softboll Forbundet
Idrottans Hus
12387 Farsta, Sweden

Swiss Baseball Softball Federation
Postfach 5
Mattenstrasse 34
4657 Dulliken, Switzerland

Rules clinic

index

Figures in *italics* indicate illustrations

index

Figures in *italics* indicate illustrations

A Ward Lock Book • Cassell • Wellington House • 125 Strand • London WC2R 0BB

A Cassell Imprint • Copyright © Ward Lock 1998
All rights reserved. No part of this book may be reproduced or transmitted in any form or by any means,
electronic or mechanical, including photocopying, recording or any information storage and retrieval system,
without prior permission in writing from the publishers and copyright owner.

Distributed in the United States by • Sterling Publishing Co. Inc. • 387 Park Avenue South • New York NY 10016 • USA

British Library Cataloguing-in-Publication Data • A catalogue record for this book is available from the British Library

ISBN 0-7063-7713-3

Designed by Grahame Dudley Associates • Illustrations by Pond & Giles • Text revisions by Ian Smyth

Printed and bound in Spain by Graficromo S.A., Cordoba